Spotlight on Social Justice

FIGHTING FOR EQUALITY

RACIAL JUSTICE IN NORTH AMERICA

NAREISSA SMITH

TWENTY-FIRST CENTURY BOOKS / MINNEAPOLIS

Dedicated to every child who wants
to create a better, more just world.
You can and will do it!

Copyright © 2025 by Lerner Publishing Group, Inc.

All rights reserved. International copyright secured. No part of this book may be reproduced, stored in a retrieval system, or transmitted in any form or by any means—electronic, mechanical, photocopying, recording, or otherwise—without the prior written permission of Lerner Publishing Group, Inc., except for the inclusion of brief quotations in an acknowledged review.

Twenty-First Century Books™
An imprint of Lerner Publishing Group, Inc.
241 First Avenue North
Minneapolis, MN 55401 USA

For reading levels and more information, look up this title at www.lernerbooks.com.

Main body text set in Bembo Std Regular
Typeface provided by Monotype Typography.

Library of Congress Cataloging-in-Publication Data

Names: Smith, Nareissa, author.
Title: Fighting for equality : racial justice in North America / Nareissa Smith.
Description: Minneapolis : Twenty-First Century Books, [2025] | Series: Spotlight on social justice | Includes bibliographical references and index. | Audience: Ages 11–18 years | Audience: Grades 7–9 | Summary: "Throughout history, many communities in North America have faced racial injustice. In response, people have worked toward legislative changes, better representation in media and government, and more. Learn about the history of racial injustice and fight for equality in North America"—Provided by publisher.
Identifiers: LCCN 2024010697 (print) | LCCN 2024010698 (ebook) | ISBN 9798765627181 (lib. bdg.) | ISBN 9798765662564 (pbk.) | ISBN 9798765659588 (epub)
Subjects: LCSH: Minorities—Civil rights—History—Juvenile literature. | Indigenous peoples—Civil rights—History—Juvenile literature. | Racism—North America—History—Juvenile literature. | Race discrimination—North America—Juvenile literature. | North America—Race relations—Juvenile literature. | Anti-racism—North America—History—Juvenile literature.
Classification: LCC JF1061 .S59 2025 (print) | LCC JF1061 (ebook) | DDC 323.173—dc23/eng/20240531

LC record available at https://lccn.loc.gov/2024010697
LC ebook record available at https://lccn.loc.gov/2024010698

Manufactured in the United States of America
1 – CG – 12/15/24

CONTENTS

INTRODUCTION ———————————————— 4

CHAPTER ONE
INDIGENOUS PEOPLES ———————————— 6

CHAPTER TWO
**THE AFRICAN DIASPORA
IN NORTH AMERICA** ———————————— 18

CHAPTER THREE
**LATINES, A NEW PEOPLE
FOR A NEW WORLD** ———————————— 32

CHAPTER FOUR
ASIANS IN NORTH AMERICA —————— 44

CONCLUSION
CREATING THE FUTURE ———————— 54

Glossary ———————————————————— 56
Source Notes ———————————————— 58
Selected Bibliography ————————— 58
Further Information —————————— 60
Index ————————————————————— 62

INTRODUCTION

To understand racial justice, it helps to understand race and justice separately. Race is the grouping together of people who share specific physical characteristics such as hair texture, skin tone, or a particular eye or nose shape. Race is different from ethnicity and nationality. Ethnicity describes a group that shares a language, history, and culture but not necessarily a race. Nationality refers to the country where a person lives or was born.

Justice is simply another word for fairness. So, saying that justice has been done is another way of saying everyone has been treated fairly.

Racial injustice occurs when people treat other groups of people differently based on their race or ethnicity. All humans have the same parts regardless of skin color or ethnic heritage. Yet some people work very hard to maintain systems of racial injustice that help some groups and hurt others. For example, at various times, the countries of North America have passed laws that treat people of color differently than white people. These laws often forced people of color to live in worse neighborhoods, go to worse schools, and generally live much harder lives.

Racial justice includes fair treatment of everyone regardless of race or ethnicity.

People of color have worked hard to change these injustices, but despite some progress, racial injustice still exists. They still face discrimination and inequality in schools, in the workplace, and in many other areas of life. Worse, the systems that maintain certain forms of racial injustice such as police brutality, housing discrimination, and voter suppression remain largely unchanged. Much work still needs to be done to achieve racial justice. Until then, racial injustice will continue to be a pressing issue.

Yet the story of people of color in North America is about more than suffering. It is also the story of people who have fought back and pressed forward despite nearly impossible odds. The following chapters will take you through the journey of several groups in North America—Indigenous peoples, people of African and Asian descent, and people with Latin American heritage. As you read, remember that racial justice isn't just history. It is an ongoing fight. Hopefully, this book will not only serve as a guide to the origins of this pursuit, but also as a tool for helping you find your place in the fight for a more equal future for everyone.

CHAPTER ONE
Indigenous Peoples

Thousands of years ago, the first humans arrived in North America. But how did they get there? They may have used a small strip of land to travel on foot between Asia and North America. They might have used boats. Or, as many Indigenous cultures teach, they may have been there from the beginning. No matter when or how they arrived, one thing is certain: Indigenous peoples lived in North America long before anyone else.

Ways of Life

Each Indigenous society approached life in its own way with its own traditions, values, government, and language. Some Indigenous peoples, such as the Lakota of now Minnesota, North Dakota, and South Dakota were nomadic. Others, including the Maya and Aztecs of present-day Mexico, developed bustling cities. Some Indigenous nations lived as hunter-gatherers, while others, such as the Hohokam of Arizona, developed complex irrigation systems that allowed them to farm even in harsh desert conditions. Some lived in portable dwellings, and some, such as the Hopi of the

American Southwest, created the first apartment-style buildings in North America. The Natchez favored monarchy, while the Haudenosaunee Confederacy of New York created one of the world's oldest democracies.

Terrace homes of the Hopi have wooden ladders connecting the rooftops. Each rooftop is the porch for the apartment above it.

What Should We Call Indigenous Peoples?

The word *Indigenous* refers to the first people to live in a particular place. So, when someone says, "the Indigenous peoples of North America," they mean the first people to live in North America. This book will use *Indigenous* when referring to multiple Indigenous groups. However, other terms have also become popular over the years in North America.

In Canada, *First Nations* refers to all Indigenous groups except the Inuit and Métis. The term *Indigenous Peoples of Canada* refers to all three groups. In Mexico, preferred terms include *comunidad* (community), *Indígena* (Indigenous), and *pueblo* (people). In the US, terms including *American Indian*, *Indian*, *Indigenous*, *Native*, and *Native American* have been used.

But when referring to a specific nation, that group's actual name should be used. It is better to say, for example, "Lakota history," "Inuit housing," or "Opata artifacts" rather than the broader term *Indigenous* because not all nations share one experience, and being specific distinguishes their individual histories. This book will also use specific terms where applicable.

Conquest and Colonization

In 1492 King Ferdinand and Queen Isabella of Spain agreed to finance Christopher Columbus's attempt to sail from Europe to Asia. On October 12, 1492, Columbus landed at Guanahani, an island in what is now the Bahamas. No one who saw the ships that day could know how much that one voyage would impact Indigenous North Americans for generations to come.

Columbus introduced slavery to the Americas. He enslaved the Lucayans and Taínos, the people who lived on the islands.

Indigenous North American Contributions to the World's Food Supply

About 60 percent of the food eaten in the modern world was developed by North American Indigenous peoples. This list of over three hundred foods includes:

- avocados
- beans
- blueberries
- chilies
- chocolate
- corn
- peanuts
- peppers
- pineapples
- pumpkins
- squash
- sweet potatoes
- tomatoes
- wild rice

The Anishinaabe used knocking sticks to harvest wild rice by knocking it into their birchbark canoes. Wild rice has more protein than most other whole grains and is a good source of antioxidants, fiber, magnesium, zinc, vitamin B-6, and niacin.

He forced them to mine for gold and dive for pearls. Those who failed to meet their monthly collection targets were maimed or killed. The attempted enslavement of North America's Indigenous peoples continued for centuries, affecting millions of them. However, in many parts of North America, Europeans found it difficult to enslave Indigenous people. This was because Indigenous groups had close allies who would help them resist the Europeans.

Columbus also opened the door to the European colonization of North America. When Columbus returned to Spain, he wrote a letter to the Spanish royals praising the islands he visited, Hispaniola and Juana (Cuba), for their fertile land, fruitful trees, and gold. Word of the letter quickly spread throughout Europe. Almost immediately, Portugal, England, and other European powers sent expeditions to what they called the New World in search of riches and new lands to claim for themselves—despite the millions of people already living there.

Some Indigenous groups successfully battled the invaders, as the Calusa of present-day Florida did when they defeated Spanish conquistador Juan Ponce De León in the early 1500s. But most nations were not able to withstand the wave of European colonizers. The Europeans had guns, but the Indigenous people did not. Though they resisted as best they could, without guns, the Indigenous people were at too great a disadvantage. Colonizers killed thousands of them. Monarchs across the ocean began claiming the lands that Indigenous peoples had called home for thousands of years.

Enslavement, dangerous weapons, and expulsion from their ancestral lands harmed and killed many Indigenous peoples. But arguably the worst blow European colonizers dealt to the population of Indigenous peoples happened accidentally. When the Europeans and their animals arrived, they brought diseases. Usually, when a person encounters a virus for the first time, special cells in their bodies fight back. If that person survives and the virus tries to attack again, their cells know how to stop it. This process is how the immune system builds immunity against certain viruses and diseases.

North America's Indigenous peoples had limited contact with Europeans for most of their history, so they didn't have many opportunities to develop immunity to diseases common in Europe but not in North America. Millions of Indigenous people died from diseases including smallpox, measles, and influenza. Typical estimates of the Indigenous population in North America before 1492 range from 15 to 112 million people. European diseases killed between 90 and 95 percent of that population. The loss devastated Indigenous societies. A loss of people meant a loss of culture. And with the Indigenous population greatly reduced, it was far easier for Europeans to colonize the remaining nations and claim their land.

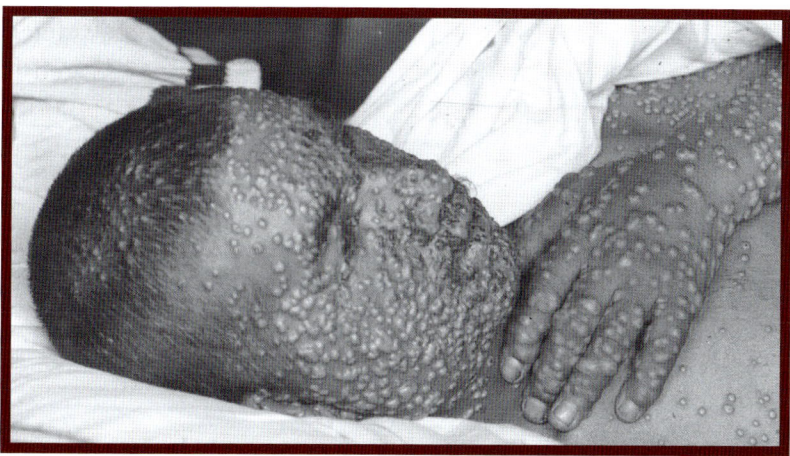

Smallpox causes high fever, body aches, and a skin rash. Many smallpox survivors have permanent scars over large areas of their bodies. Smallpox can also cause blindness.

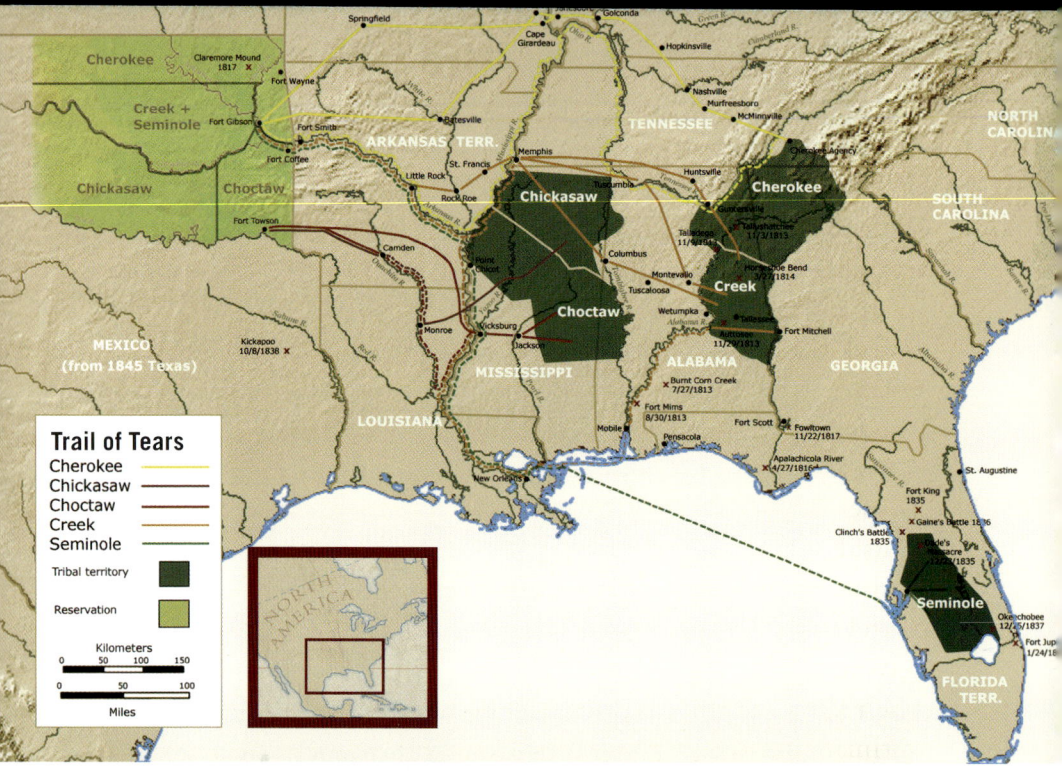

The Trail of Tears had many different routes and spanned more than 5,000 miles (8,047 km) over land and water.

The US Indian Removal Act

In the early 1800s many European settlers in the US and Canada began to declare that it was God's will for white settlers to conquer North America. This belief, now known as Manifest Destiny, caused these settlers to pressure their governments to make more western land available for them to live on and farm.

The resulting drive west endangered the Indigenous peoples who already lived in these regions. The US government wanted their land to be given to settlers. The government passed the Indian Removal Act in 1830. The law said that Indigenous people who lived east of the Mississippi River and agreed to give up their ancestral lands would be taken to unsettled western territories to live there instead.

However, *agreed* isn't completely accurate. President Andrew Jackson's secretary of war said that if any nations refused to turn over their land, "the President . . . would march an army into their country." These threats of violence were effective, and groups including the Chickasaw, Choctaw, Creek, and Seminole left their homes between 1831 and 1835. They walked thousands of miles from the eastern US to modern-day Oklahoma. This journey was known as the Trail of Tears. Many people died along the way from preventable causes such as starvation, disease, and being forced to sleep outside in cold and wet conditions. The Cherokee Nation resisted longer, but in 1838 the US government forced over sixteen thousand Cherokee people to walk the Trail of Tears. Overall, 100 thousand Indigenous people were forced from their land, and about fifteen thousand died. Most experts estimate between three thousand and six thousand people who died were Cherokee.

Indigenous peoples also lost their ancestral lands in wars. For example, the United States secured major parts of present-day Alabama and Florida by waging and winning wars against the Creek and Seminole peoples. Indigenous nations won some battles over land, as the Oglala and Cheyenne did when they defeated US General George Custer's forces at the Battle of the Little Bighorn in present-day Montana. But it wasn't enough to stop the loss of land. The US government also began creating reservations in the 1850s, further forcing Indigenous peoples off their land and into smaller regions while also removing much of their political power.

Ancestral land is crucial to Indigenous cultures. When land was lost, the people who had lived on it for centuries lost the places where they hunted, farmed, raised their families, buried their loved ones, and more. Losing land also meant the loss of culture.

REFLECT

Why does knowing that Indigenous people were the first people in North America matter?

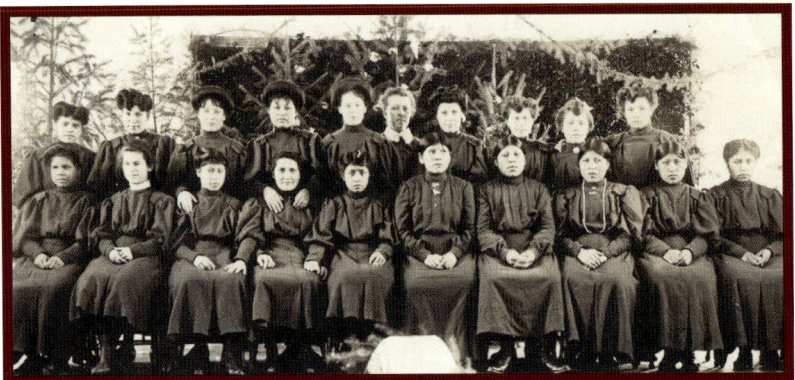

The Fort Spokane Boarding School near Spokane, Washington, operated from 1900 to 1914. Besides going to school, Indigenous students at Fort Spokane were forced to sew their own clothes, repair sheets and curtains, plant their own crops, and work in the kitchen.

Culture

Forcibly removing Indigenous peoples from and taking their land was not the only way that North American governments harmed Indigenous nations. Many people in the US and Canada believed that Indigenous people should reject their cultures and behave more like white Europeans. Their governments created policies designed to wipe out Indigenous cultures. One common saying at the time was, "Kill the Indian in him, and save the man." This meant that Indigenous people would be permitted to live alongside white people if they rejected their traditions and fully embraced white culture. This is called cultural assimilation. White people often forced Indigenous people to assimilate. Some of their most harmful methods involved children.

Both the US and Canada adopted child removal policies. Starting in the 1950s, if a white social worker believed an Indigenous family could not care for a child for any reason, they would remove the child from their home and place them with white foster parents. In Canada, over twenty thousand First Nations children were taken from their homes between the 1950s and 1980s.

The US and Canadian governments also created boarding schools for Indigenous children in the 1800s. At these schools, Indigenous children were forced to give up their names, hair, clothing, religious beliefs, and any other ties to their culture. Students who tried to keep their traditions alive were punished, beaten, or severely abused. At least four thousand Canadian First Nations boarding school students died between 1870 and 1996 from accidents, disease, and abuse. Between 1819 and 1969, five hundred Indigenous children died in boarding schools across the US too.

The students who survived also suffered. When they returned home, they no longer knew their original language or customs. Most students found it hard to fit in with their Indigenous families, friends, and communities. Many carried the trauma caused by abuse and separation from their families with them throughout their lives.

Current Issues

Enslavement, land loss, forced assimilation, and other harmful policies are all examples of the racial injustice Indigenous people have faced throughout history. While many of these systems have ended, Indigenous people across North America still face injustice.

Indigenous people are more likely to live in poverty than white people. Several complex factors contribute to the ongoing poverty among many Indigenous communities in North America. These include limited access to economic opportunities because of living in remote reservation areas

On March 10, 2017, in Washington, DC, Indigenous people from many nations protested and marched against the Dakota Access Pipeline. The pipeline transports oil from North Dakota to Illinois, running through important cultural and burial sites in the Standing Rock Reservation and other Indigenous nations. The pipeline also crosses under the Mississippi and Missouri Rivers, so some people are concerned that an oil spill could contaminate drinking water.

and underfunded schools. Also, there are still attempts to take, use, or harm Indigenous lands, such as by running oil pipelines through them, which can end up contaminating the water supply and the soil in which food is grown.

But there has been progress toward justice too. In the 1960s First Nations and Indigenous American campaigns such as the American Indian Movement and the National Indian Brotherhood (now the Assembly of First Nations) began working to expose and fight against assimilation policies such as child removal. Throughout the twenty-first century, activists have organized protests and other events to help protect Indigenous lands from pipelines and overuse.

The Land Back Movement, led by Indigenous peoples, advocates for returning Indigenous lands back to their stewardship. Encouraged by this movement, a growing number of individuals, businesses, universities, and governments are taking steps to acknowledge that they sit on Indigenous lands and identify the peoples who originally lived there. Indigenous activists have also advocated for and convinced some major sports teams and brands to stop using names and images that belittle Indigenous peoples and their cultures.

In the 2020s Indigenous Americans are breaking political barriers too. Deb Haaland is the first Indigenous woman to serve as a US Cabinet Secretary, holding the Secretary of the Interior position since 2021. Before this, she served as a congresswoman from New Mexico, advocating for environmental protection and Indigenous rights. Sharice Davids was elected to the US Congress in 2018. She is a member of the Ho-Chunk Nation. Peggy Flanagan became the first Indigenous woman elected Lieutenant Governor of a US state in 2018. She is a member of the White Earth band of Ojibwe and advocates for issues such as education, health care, and Indigenous rights.

Despite these encouraging signs, there is still far too much injustice. Land acknowledgments are a start but do not give Indigenous communities their ancestral lands back or money for community resources such as schools. While Indigenous Americans are making strides in US politics, certain voting laws are working to prevent them from exercising their full political power. Some states have enacted laws that ban the use of tribal IDs for voter identification, which limits the ability of Indigenous people to participate in elections. Some reservations also don't have any polling places, forcing Indigenous voters to drive more than 100 miles (161 km) each way to vote. Until all injustices are corrected, the work must continue.

REFLECT
What do you think racial justice would look like for North American Indigenous people?

CHAPTER TWO
The African Diaspora in North America

Usually, when people move from one country to another, they decide to do so on their own. This was not the case for many Africans in North America. With few exceptions, Africans first came to North America against their will. Europeans sailed to Africa, kidnapped Africans, and brought them to North and South America, including Brazil, Jamaica, and the United States, to be enslaved. A diaspora is a group of people residing far from their ancestral homelands. The African diaspora has a strong presence in North America, mostly because of enslavement. African descendants make up roughly 2 percent of Mexico's population, 4 percent of Canada's, and 14 percent of the United States's.

Though these Africans had no choice in coming to North America, once they arrived, they and their descendants did their best to make a home in the new land. Although they lived and worked in dangerous conditions, over time, their tenacity and will to survive improved conditions not only for themselves, but for everyone.

Life in Africa

To understand the racial injustice African people and their descendants face in modern North America, it helps to understand the injustice they faced when they first arrived. When people tell that story, it usually begins with them arriving in a new world. While this did happen, Afro-Mexicans, African Americans, and Afro-Canadians cannot be fully understood without the stories of their ancestors.

   Long before the slave trade began in the early 1500s, Africa contained great societies. Empires flourished. For example, the empire of Mali was known for its wealth, and its leader from 1312 to 1337, Mansa Musa, is considered the richest man to have ever lived. Beyond material wealth, Mali was also home to advanced architecture, libraries, and universities.

   Like Indigenous Americans, ancient African cultures and traditions were too many and too complex to lump together. The important point is that these ancient Africans had cultures. They had traditions, religions, languages, art styles, families, homes, and people and communities that they loved.

   After Columbus' journey to the Americas, European countries rushed to establish colonies there to use the land's resources. But to do that, they needed people to work the land. Enslaving Indigenous peoples didn't work. So, in need of a larger workforce than the colonies provided, the Europeans turned to Africa in the 1600s. Unlike Indigenous peoples, Africans had some immunity to European diseases. This made them suitable to work in North America—even if they didn't want to.

What Do We Call the Descendants of Africans?

When discussing Africans in North America, the preferred terms have changed many times. After the Civil War (1861–1865), the term *Colored* became popular. By the 1940s *Negro* had replaced *Colored*.

Up to this point, the word *Black* was seen as negative. But the Black Power movement of the 1960s encouraged people of African descent to embrace the word *Black* as beautiful. The movement also encouraged the African diaspora to reconnect with Africa positively, so terms like *Afro-Canadian* and *Afro-American* came into use at this time. By the 1990s *African American* became a common preferred term in the US. *Black* also remains very popular there and in Canada. This book will use terms such as *African American*, *Afro-Canadian*, or *Afro-Mexican* to recognize and honor the importance of the diaspora's African origins.

While *Negro* and *Colored* might appear in historical documents or the names of long-established organizations, such as in this 1941 National Association for the Advancement of Colored People (NAACP) poster, these terms should not be used to refer to people of African descent because they are now considered outdated and offensive.

Trading in People

Captured people were marched hundreds or thousands of miles to Africa's Atlantic Coast. Then they were forced to wait in dungeons for as long as a year until a ship arrived. Once it did, the people were packed in the boat's dark, damp cargo hold and shackled together. They could not move unless unshackled, not even to go to the bathroom.

They remained this way for the entire journey from Africa to North America, a trip that could take three months. Historians call this voyage the Middle Passage. Knowing how many people endured the Middle Passage is difficult due to very little and poor documentation. Most experts estimate it to be between ten and fifteen million people.

European nations developed a process called the Triangular Trade. European traders loaded their ships with products and sailed to Africa. Once there, they traded items in exchange for humans. Then they sailed to North America with these humans. The European traders sold the newly enslaved people at auctions. The Europeans then bought items with the money they made. They sailed back to Europe with these items, sold them, and restarted the whole process.

Olaudah Equiano Describes the Middle Passage

Olaudah Equiano (also known as Gustavus Vassa) was an enslaved man who learned to read and write. In his 1789 book, *The Interesting Narrative of the Life of Olaudah Equiano*, he said about the Middle Passage:

> "... [T]he whole ship's cargo were confined together, it became absolutely pestilential [harmful]. The closeness of the place, and the heat of the climate, added to the number in the ship, which was so crowded that each had scarcely room to turn himself, almost suffocated us. This produced copious perspirations [fumes], so that the air soon became unfit for respiration [breathing], from a variety of loathsome smells, and brought on a sickness among the slaves, of which many died ..."

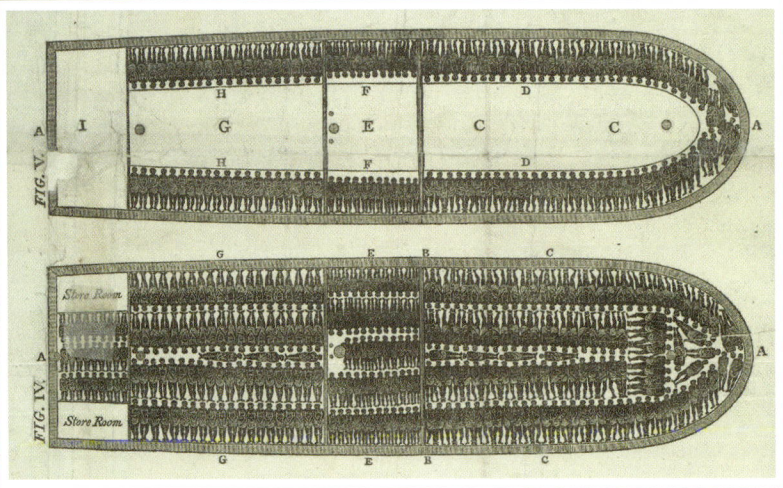

The Brookes ship transported enslaved Africans to the Caribbean. Knowing that many enslaved people would die on the three-month trip, traders would pack as many people as possible onto the ship. This diagram depicts four hundred enslaved people, but the ship could carry around six hundred.

Enslavement

Each North American region had its own approach to enslavement. Mexico's Catholic tradition required that it give enslaved people certain rights, such as the right to marry and the right to be free from cruel treatment. But in reality, these rights were not always enforced. And no matter how many "rights" they were given, these enslaved Africans had no true freedom.

Slavery in the US and Canada was even harsher. Enslaved people worked from "can't see in the morning until can't see at night." Working and living conditions were so hard that the average enslaved person in Canada died at the age of twenty-five. Although they worked all day in dangerous conditions, their enslavers paid them nothing.

Enslaved people in Canada and the US also had no rights. In the US, enslaved people could not marry. It was illegal for them to learn to read or write and for large groups of Africans to gather except for church services. Those who broke these rules could be punished. One common punishment was beating the "rule-breaker" with a whip designed for livestock.

But worse than physical punishment was the fact that the enslaved people were legal property, with no more rights than a chair. This meant that they could be sold at any time for any reason. Enslavers would often punish Africans who tried to talk back, fight, or resist their living and work conditions in any way by selling their children, parents, or other loved ones. The fear of losing their families was a powerful motivator for enslaved people to follow even the most unjust rules.

Still, enslaved Africans did their best to fight back against the injustice they faced. Some fought back in highly visible ways, such as running away to freedom. Others resisted in smaller ways such as learning to read, teaching others to read, working slowly, or destroying things. Even these small acts of defiance helped enslaved people maintain their dignity.

Eventually, each country in North America ended slavery. Mexico and Canada legally abolished slavery in 1829 and 1834, respectively. But it took the Civil War to end slavery in the US. The anti-slavery northern Union fought the pro-slavery southern Confederacy. The Union won, and the US government abolished slavery in 1865.

Post-Slavery

Although slavery had ended, white North Americans would not stand side by side with the Africans. They created unjust segregation laws. These were sometimes called Jim Crow laws in the US, after a racist character white people used to mock African American people. Some segregated places included schools, movie theaters, parks, public pools, neighborhoods, hospitals, and cemeteries.

In addition to segregation, Canada and the US restricted African people from voting. Though Canada protected the voting rights of Afro-Canadians in theory, there was a condition: only those who owned property could vote. Most Afro-Canadians were ultimately excluded because it had been illegal during slavery for Afro-Canadians to own property, and, newly freed, they didn't have the money to buy any. In the US, many southern states required people to pass literacy tests before voting. But because it had been illegal to teach enslaved people to read and write, few African Americans knew how to, making it difficult or even impossible to pass.

African Americans also faced physical violence. In the South, white people who were resentful of the African

A person drinking at a segregated water cooler in Oklahoma City, Oklahoma, in 1939. The Civil Rights Act of 1964 officially ended segregation of public places, including water fountains and restrooms.

Americans' new freedom and legal rights attacked them. Sometimes, they lynched African Americans. A lynching is a public killing without a trial. Sometimes, they burned down African American neighborhoods and businesses. Any African American who dared to challenge any white person or segregation might be targeted. For example, in Tulsa, Oklahoma, in 1921, a group of white people attacked the prosperous African American area known as Black Wall

Street. They destroyed nearly $2 million worth of property, and three hundred African Americans were killed.

In response to the discriminatory laws and treatment, African Americans and Afro-Canadians fought for justice in many ways. African Americans started organizations such as the NAACP, founded in 1909, to protest lynching and demand equal rights. While they did not win immediately, their fight paved the way for civil rights movements.

Civil Rights

Laws that protect people from unjust treatment are often called civil rights laws. African Americans and Afro-Canadians pushed hard for these laws. Canada's civil rights movement, the Rights Revolution, lasted from 1945 to 1982, pushing Canada to pass laws protecting Afro-Canadians.

The US Civil Rights Movement began in the 1950s. In 1954 the US Supreme Court decided *Brown v. Board of Education*, a case that challenged segregation in public schools. The judges ruled that separating children in public schools based on race violated the US Constitution and was therefore illegal.

In August 1955 thirteen-year-old Emmet Till was killed after he allegedly whistled at or otherwise "disrespected" a white woman. The woman's family lynched Till and threw his body in a river. Till's mother, Mamie, decided to display her son's body in an open casket to expose the cruelty African American people faced in hopes of ending it. Members of Till's family testified against the white men who killed him although they knew they could be attacked next. The bravery that Till's family showed by allowing his body to be displayed in an open casket and testifying publicly against his attackers inspired a new confidence in African Americans.

Another figure helped inspire African Americans too. On December 1, 1955, Rosa Parks, a seamstress in Montgomery, Alabama, refused to move when a bus driver ordered her to give her seat to a white passenger. Parks was arrested. Outraged, the Black women of Montgomery organized a bus boycott overnight. As the boycott gained national attention, a young preacher named Reverend Dr. Martin Luther King Jr. became one of the most visible leaders of the new Civil Rights Movement. King and his associates led successful campaigns for new laws that ended segregation in public places (the Civil Rights Act of 1964), granted African Americans more voting rights (the Voting Rights Act of 1965), and forbade housing discrimination (the Fair Housing Act of 1968). These laws changed the US forever.

King and his partners adopted a strict policy of nonviolence because King believed that violence would only lead to more violence. But other leaders, such as Malcolm X, said that African Americans were within their

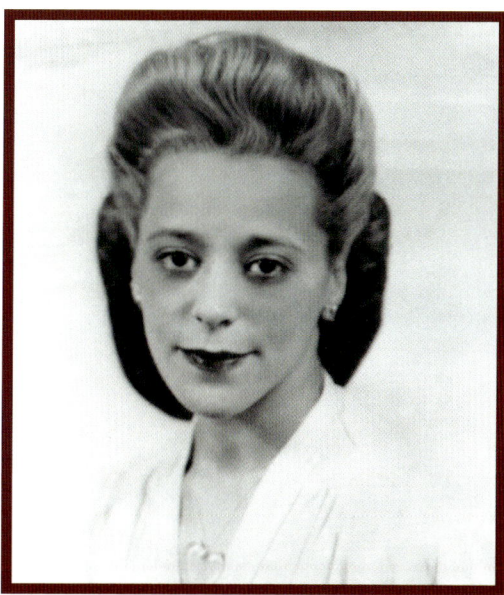

Viola Desmond (*pictured*) was kicked out of a Canadian theater because she refused to sit in the segregated section in 1946. Her friend Carrie Best had been evicted from the same theater five years earlier for the same reason. They both sued the theater. Neither woman won their case in court, but their actions were major parts of Canada's Rights Revolution.

legal rights to use force in self-defense against white violence. Malcolm X's words inspired the Black Power movement, which focused on helping develop Black neighborhoods and businesses. Black Power groups such as the Black Panthers also created health and education programs to help their communities.

> **REFLECT**
> **What are the pros and cons of King's strict use of nonviolence? Do you think violence is sometimes necessary to effect change? Why or why not?**

Current Issues

African Americans have made major gains since the Civil Rights Movement. For example, in 1968 just over half of African American students finished high school. By 2018 that number had grown to over 90 percent. African Americans' average incomes have also increased.

African Americans have made political gains as well. Barack Obama became the first African American US president in 2009. Kamala Harris became the first African American US vice president in 2021. In 2023 African Americans had the most representation of any people of color in Congress.

However, much still needs to be achieved. Though segregation is officially over, many schools and neighborhoods are still very segregated by both race and class in the US. Several court decisions, such as *Shelby County v. Holder* in 2013, which invalidated part of the Voting Rights Act that King and others worked so hard to secure, have made it more difficult for African Americans to vote. And years of enslavement without pay, employment discrimination, and lack of education opportunities

King was assassinated in Memphis, Tennessee, in April 1968. He was thirty-nine years old.

Zion Cash (*center*) gets help tying a necktie during the Empowering Males to Build Opportunities for Developing Independence Summit at Elon University in North Carolina in 2012. The Delta Sigma Theta Sorority holds these summits across the US to help young African American men prepare for professional careers.

contribute to a persistent, generational wealth gap between white people and African Americans.

The issue is not just in the US. Throughout North America, African descendants are far more likely to live in poverty than white people. And in each country, police violence targets people of African descent. Groups such as Black Lives Matter are fighting back against police violence by tracking police actions and demanding accountability.

Activists and organizations are also fighting for justice in other areas. The NAACP and the NAACP Legal Defense Fund work to protect voting rights and other civil rights. While official organizations do great work, for centuries, African Americans have used their fraternities, sororities, churches, clubs, and other community organizations to respond to the injustices in their communities. In 2020 activists protested the Confederate flag's placement at the South Carolina state capitol because, for many people, the flag symbolizes slavery and racial discrimination. Though a state law prevented the flag from being removed, an African American woman named Bree Newsome climbed the pole and removed the flag. She was arrested, but the flag was later removed for good.

> **REFLECT**
>
> **Some US states such as California and New York are considering paying reparations to the descendants of Africans who were enslaved. Reparations are money that a government pays to right a wrong. Do you think reparations for slavery is a good idea? Why or why not?**

CHAPTER THREE
Latines, a New People for a New World

Because Spain colonized most of the countries Latines come from, most Latines have a similar or shared language, culture, and history. Since Latines do not belong to any one racial group and share a common background, experts usually refer to Latines as an ethnic group rather than a race. However, much like other people of color in North America, many Latine people have been singled out or faced discrimination because of their skin color and shared cultural characteristics.

Latines—A History of Movement

Latines make up nineteen percent of the US population. But how did the first US Latines become US citizens? Because Spain sponsored Columbus' voyage, Spain was heavily involved in colonizing North America from the start. Spain's prized colony in North America was New Spain, founded in 1535. In 1821 New Spain won a ten-year war for independence from Spain and became Mexico.

The state of Texas was originally part of Mexico. In 1836 it declared its independence. Texas operated as an

The first major battle of the Mexican-American War was the Battle of Palo Alto. It took place near the modern city of Brownsville, Texas.

independent nation for several years before it became the twenty-eighth US state in 1845. Texas becoming a part of the United States angered the Mexican government. In May 1846 the Mexican-American War (1846–1848) began. After Mexico surrendered, the two countries signed the Treaty of Guadalupe Hildago. Under that treaty, Mexico agreed to give Texas to the United States. Mexico also gave the US 525,000 square miles (1,359,743 sq. km) of land covering present-day Arizona, California, Colorado, Nevada, New Mexico, Utah, and Wyoming. Almost overnight, roughly 115 thousand Mexicans became US citizens.

What's the Difference between Hispanic and Latino?

The word *Hispanic* focuses on language rather than geography. A Spanish-speaking person from Spain, Mexico, or another Spanish-speaking country is considered Hispanic. However, a person from Brazil is not because most Brazilians speak Portuguese.

Latino comes from Latin America, which refers to countries in Mexico, Central America, South America, and the islands of the Caribbean. *Latino* refers to all people who are or whose ancestors are Latin American. For example, someone from Spain would not be considered Latino, but Brazilians and Haitians would be because those countries are part of Latin America.

You may have also heard the term *Latinx*. Spanish nouns are masculine or feminine. In Spanish, *Latinos* is considered masculine but is often used to signify both all-male groups and groups of people of multiple or unknown genders. But using a masculine word to describe everyone can leave out people who aren't men. Because of this, LGBTQ+ Spanish-speakers coined *Latinx* and *Latine* as gender-neutral terms to describe Latinos. This book will use *Latine* throughout to include as many members of this community as possible.

Latin American countries are in two shades of green. Countries in which Spanish or Portuguese is not the official language are shaded in the light green.

FIGHTING FOR EQUALITY

Spanish-American War

Other Latines became US citizens in a similar way. In 1898 a US ship near the Spanish colony of Cuba was attacked. The United States accused Spain of bombing the ship. The Spanish-American War (1898) began, and the US quickly won. At the end of the war, Spain and the US signed the Treaty of Paris. Spain gave the US control of Cuba, Puerto Rico, Guam, and the Philippines. Puerto Rico and Guam became US territories. Puerto Ricans became US citizens in 1917, and the people of Guam became US citizens in 1950.

Latine Immigration to Canada

For decades, Canada was under British rule and didn't have its own colonies. Without colonies, Canada couldn't establish connections with Latin countries through colonialism. Instead, it had to rely on immigration, when people move to a new country.

Latine immigration to Canada progressed slowly. It wasn't until the early 1970s that waves of Latine immigrants began arriving in the country as they fled wars and unrest in their home countries. In 1970 there were fewer than 3 thousand Latines in Canada. By 2023 that number had increased to 1.2 million.

Dancers perform during the 2017 Salsa on St. Clair Street Festival in Toronto, Canada. It is one of the largest Latine festivals in Canada.

Making a New Home

In the Treaty of Guadalupe Hildago, the US promised to honor Mexican citizens' land rights. But in reality, these people were living in a new land that used laws they didn't know and a language they didn't speak. It was difficult to protect their land in court. Many Latines lost their land. Losing their land and the income it provided meant they lost large amounts of money over the years. Losing this money meant it could not be passed down to the next generation, contributing to modern Latines often holding less generational wealth than white North Americans.

Social Injustices

Many people immigrated to the US from Mexico during the Mexican Revolution (1910–1920) to avoid the violence of war. As the number of Mexican Americans grew, many white Americans tried to stop Mexican immigrants from standing up for themselves or exercising their rights. This often happened through violence. Around five thousand Mexican immigrants were shot, hanged, whipped, or burned alive between 1910 and 1920. And most of them were US citizens.

Mexican Americans could not complain about the violence and discrimination to law enforcement because law enforcement groups sometimes participated in the violence. For example, on December 25, 1917, several white people were killed at the Brite Ranch in Texas. The Texas Rangers, a law enforcement agency, investigated the crime. They accused Mexican Americans from the town of Porvenir of committing the murders. But Porvenir was 40 miles (64 km) from Brite Ranch, and no roads connected them. No one could prove that anyone from Porvenir had committed these murders. But the next month, the Rangers rounded up fifteen Mexican American men and boys in Porvenir and shot and killed them. Then, they burned the town to the ground.

This incident was one of many that Mexican Americans and other Latine communities faced. Dealing with constant attacks and discrimination from citizens and law enforcement alike made it difficult for these communities to live in safety.

Like African Americans, Latines experienced segregation. They attended segregated schools, which often lacked teachers or equipment. Some schools did not even offer to teach all grades. Latines were also prevented from using the same restaurants, movie theaters, or restrooms as white people.

Laws also restricted Latines from voting. Many states that required literacy tests only provided them in English, making it difficult for Spanish speakers who knew little or no English to pass them. That made it more difficult for Latines to vote and therefore harder to fully participate in national life.

Immigration laws throughout history have greatly affected

Longino Flores (*framed portrait*) was one of the men killed in the Porvenir Massacre. In June 1918 the governor of Texas fired or reassigned several rangers who had been involved in the massacre.

LATINES, A NEW PEOPLE FOR A NEW WORLD

Latines coming to the US. Much of the Latine immigration story involves attempts to keep Latines out.

In the 1930s the US government deported 1.8 million Mexican Americans to Mexico to preserve jobs and resources for white citizens. Then in the 1950s the US began a program designed to catch people who had migrated to the country without documentation or government approval. However, the program was so big and unregulated that some people deported to Mexico were US citizens.

Fighting Back

Latines have faced many challenges, but they have not backed down. They created organizations to protect and increase their rights and fight against segregation. Founded in 1929, the League of United Latin American Citizens worked hard to end segregation. The league also took important legal actions, such as suing school boards that ran segregated schools.

Latines were also heavily involved in the labor movement from its beginning in the nineteenth century. Factory and farm laborers worked hard, but their bosses often treated them poorly. The laborers frequently worked long hours in dangerous conditions for little pay. They joined together to ask for better pay, safer conditions, and shorter work hours. The workers used methods such as boycotts, marches, and strikes to improve their conditions. Over time, the labor movement would help create laws that protected all workers by demanding higher pay, safer conditions, and more worker benefits such as health care.

Latines also created and joined many worker unions that helped change working conditions. In 1903 Latine Americans and Japanese Americans started one of the first multiracial farm workers unions, the Japanese-Mexican Labor

Association. This union was among the first to convince powerful agricultural companies to agree to workers' requests for higher pay. In 1905 Lucy Gonzales Parsons, an Afro-Latine woman, helped start another labor movement group called the Industrial Workers of the World. This group was committed to helping workers and promoting social and economic justice. She was the only woman to speak at the group's founding convention.

Parsons led protest picket lines and spoke about workers' rights around the US.

Latine Youth Activism

Organizing and activism are not just for adults. In 1968 over ten thousand Latine high school students across Los Angeles walked out of their classes. They organized the walkout to protest being punished for speaking Spanish at school and discouraged from attending college. The walkout lasted one week, eventually spreading to one hundred schools in ten states. Although the students could not get their school districts to stop the unfair treatment immediately, they inspired others to act.

In 1969 Puerto Rican students in Chicago formed the Young Lords Organization. Like the Black Panthers, the Young Lords focused on providing their community with political education, food, and health care. They created a "patients' bill of rights" that inspired the documents that hospitals still use to ensure patients are treated respectfully, have treatments explained, and can pick their own doctors.

During the 1960s and 1970s, Latine students also created a movement to ensure teachers taught Latine history. The students succeeded in introducing Chicano studies programs at schools such as the University of Texas at Austin and the University of California, Los Angeles. *Chicano* is a term Mexican Americans created and use to describe Americans with Mexican heritage.

Youth at the Marcha por la Justicia (March for Justice) on January 31, 1971. They were protesting police brutality in South Central Los Angeles.

Chavez (*pictured*) and Huerta used nonviolent tactics to lobby for farm workers' rights.

Latines continued to be at the forefront of securing workers' rights for decades. In 1965 Dolores Huerta and Cesar Chavez founded the United Farm Workers Union. This union, which was created to help migrant farm workers, achieved many important goals including securing contracts that guaranteed workers breaks, bathrooms, health care, and parental leave.

REFLECT

Why do you think Latines played important leadership roles in the labor movement?

Current Issues

As of the 2020s Latines in Canada are rapidly moving into more high-paying professional jobs. The same is true in the US, where the percentage of Latines in professional occupations jumped from 8 percent to 11 percent between 2012 and 2022. Latines in the US are more likely to finish high school or complete college than ever before. From 2012 to 2022, Latines who completed high school rose from 75 to 88 percent. And the number of Latines with college degrees jumped from 15 to 25 percent.

Latines are also breaking barriers and making a difference in their communities. Sonia Sotomayor is the first Latina to serve on the United States Supreme Court, becoming a Supreme Court Justice in 2009. She has played a crucial role in shaping federal legal decisions that impact racial justice issues including increasing equal rights and opportunities. Besides creating the hit musical *Hamilton*, actor and composer Lin-Manuel Miranda has used his work to shed light on issues of race, social justice, and immigration.

However, challenges remain. Latines in Canada and the US still face high dropout rates in school compared to other groups. In the US, the Latine dropout rate is still nearly twice the rate for white students. Some organizations, including the Latin American Association, Hispanic Federation, and the Council of Mexican Federations in North America, are actively working to address dropout rates in the US and Canada by providing college advising and prep courses, summer education, and mentoring programs.

Latines are also often at the center of the immigration debate. Even though over 80 percent of Latines in the US are citizens, anti–immigration politicians often make discriminatory comments that lump all Latines together and portray them poorly.

Many Latine individuals are advocating against discriminatory comments and policies targeting immigrant communities. Through his work as a journalist, filmmaker, and activist, Jose Antonio Vargas has

Right to left: Sotomayor, walking with then president Barack Obama and vice president Joe Biden, was born in the Bronx, New York. Her parents were from Puerto Rico.

FIGHTING FOR EQUALITY

United We Dream is the largest immigrant youth-led organization in the US. It fights discrimination and xenophobia through marches, know-your-rights workshops, and public education, and by using social media and storytelling to amplify the voices of immigrant youth. In 2021 members protested in Washington, DC to demand an end to deportations.

helped to humanize the issue of immigration and challenge the stereotypes of immigrants. Erika Andiola co-founded the Dream Action Coalition, which advocates for legislative solutions to protect undocumented youth and their families. She has been a vocal advocate for protecting the rights of immigrant youth and speaking out against discrimination and xenophobia.

Latines in Canada and the US are one of the fastest-growing populations in North America. This growth will create more cultural diversity and opportunities for political and social representation in the future. With increasing numbers, Latines have become an influential political force, causing politicians to pay attention to their issues and concerns. Latines will undoubtedly play a role in shaping the future of North America.

CHAPTER FOUR
Asians in North America

In 1587 a Spanish ship set sail from China to North America. Its crew included eight sailors from the Philippines. When the sailors landed in what is now Morro Bay, California, they became the first Asians to arrive in North America.

Over the next centuries, Asians established themselves in every part of North America. By the 1600s there were many Chinese people in Mexico City. In 1763 Filipinos founded the first Asian American settlement, Saint Malo, in what is now the US state of Louisiana. In 1788 fifty Chinese artisans established a trading post in Vancouver's Nootka Sound.

Even more Asian people arrived in North America in the 1800s. In the 1850s gold was discovered in British Columbia, Canada. Dreams of riches, especially gold, enticed some Asians. By 1858 Chinese migrants looking to join in the search for gold helped establish Barkerville, British Columbia, Canada's first Chinese community.

Around the same time, the California gold rush brought many Chinese people to the US. And as the US gained land in the West, it needed a way to get people there. Completing the Transcontinental Railroad was one of the US government's top priorities. The railroad was designed to

A camp for Chinese workers along the Transcontinental Railroad. In addition to being paid less than white workers, Chinese workers experienced segregation and had to pay for their own supplies.

connect eastern America to the Pacific coast. Building the railroad was difficult work that involved explosions, avalanches, and extreme cold. Although they were paid one-third less than white workers, many Chinese immigrants were willing to do dangerous work to support themselves and their families in this new land.

Limiting Asian Rights

Asians worked hard to support the countries they called home. By 1870 Chinese immigrants were just 0.02 percent of the total US population but 20 percent of California's workforce. But not everyone appreciated their hard work and contributions.

As more Asian immigrants arrived in North America, they faced discrimination. In Canada, less than fifteen years after Chinese immigrants helped establish the town of Barkerville, British Columbia changed the voting law to restrict Chinese Canadian men from voting. By 1885

Barkerville, British Columbia, was one of North America's first established Chinese communities. During the mid-1860s gold rush, half of Barkerville's population was Chinese. The town is now a living history museum with one of the largest Chinese archival collections in Canada.

Canada's government had created a "head tax." The tax required Chinese migrants to pay a fee before entering the country. No other groups were required to pay the tax except for the Chinese immigrants. This discriminatory tax was part of a broader pattern of discrimination and anti-Chinese bias in Canada. The Chinese Exclusion Act replaced the head tax in 1923. It completely banned Chinese immigration to Canada until it was repealed in 1947.

Things were no better in the US. In 1882 Congress passed the Chinese Exclusion Act. This law made it difficult for Chinese people to enter the US. The law also said that Chinese immigrants could not become US citizens. Later, the law changed to require Chinese and Chinese Americans to carry special certificates that proved they could legally live in the US. Those who failed to show their certificates could be jailed or deported unless a "credible white witness" explained that they could legally live in the country.

During World War I (1914–1918), the US Congress created the Immigration Act of 1917. Politicians were worried about national security during the war and thought limiting immigration from certain regions would increase national defense. This law limited immigration not only from China, but also from Burma (modern-day Myanmar), India, Malaysia, and Thailand. Next, the US government passed the Immigration Act of 1924, which favored Western and Northern European immigration while restricting immigration from Asia even more.

Asian Is a Broad Term

Asia is the world's largest continent and contains forty-eight countries. Each Asian nation has its own unique culture. And Asians practice many different customs and religions, even in the same country. So, the term *Asian* is too broad to explain the rich, individual contributions that each Asian culture has made to North America.

On the other hand, the term *Asian* can be unifying. Many Asians in North America share some experiences. In the US, about half of all Asians are the children or grandchildren of immigrants. Also, many Asian North Americans share the experience of being discriminated against or treated as outsiders. While *Asian* is not a perfect term, it can help people bond over their shared experiences.

So, this book will use *Asians* when referring to Asians in more than one North American country. It will also use specific terms such as *Asian Canadian* or *Chinese American* whenever possible.

Multiple generations of Japanese Americans ate together at mealtime in the Manzanar Incarceration Camp in California.

The treatment of Asian Americans worsened when World War II (1939–1945) began. In 1939 German dictator Adolf Hitler ordered his troops to invade Poland. Shortly after, Britain and France declared war on Germany, sparking World War II. Germany's primary allies in the war were Italy and Japan.

On April 7, 1941, Japan attacked Pearl Harbor, a US military post in Hawaii. The US declared war on Japan. Americans feared that Japanese Americans, especially those who lived on the West Coast, would support Japan in the war. There was no evidence to support this claim. Many Japanese Americans supported US war efforts and had little connection to Japan.

But in 1942 US president Franklin D. Roosevelt signed an order that allowed the US military to gather Japanese Americans and imprison them in incarceration camps. This order

REFLECT

Do you believe paying reparations to Japanese American citizens who were detained in incarceration camps during World War II is a fair form of justice? Why or why not?

imprisoned 120 thousand Japanese Americans. The camps were cold and unsanitary, so diseases spread quickly. Canada's and Mexico's militaries also operated Japanese incarceration camps.

Reparations for Japanese American Incarceration

Japanese Americans who were incarcerated lost their jobs, property, homes, and businesses. Eventually, Canada, Mexico, and the US paid reparations to Japanese citizens who were sent to the camps. Mexico paid reparations in 1957, but it took the US and Canada more than forty years after they entered the war to apologize and pay reparations. They did so in 1988.

Impacts of the Vietnam War

During the 1960s as African Americans began pushing for civil rights, Asian Americans were inspired to do the same. But in 1965 the US joined the Vietnam War (1954–1975). The Vietnam War began in 1954 when Vietnam was split into two parts, North Vietnam and South Vietnam. North Vietnam supported communism while South Vietnam opposed it. The US, which was anti-communist, helped South Vietnam and fought against North Vietnam.

Asian Americans watched the Vietnam War unfold on the news. They realized that if Vietnamese people were painted as the enemy on the news, it would be easy to paint all Asians in the US as the enemy at home as well. And that happened. Some Asian Americans faced verbal and physical abuse regardless of their nationality. Some people unfairly questioned Asian American people's loyalty to the United States. Asian Americans were the victims of assaults, harassment, and vandalism.

Of the 8.7 million US soldiers who served in the Vietnam War, about thirty-five thousand were Asian American. Some Asian American soldiers faced harsh discrimination including getting beat up, called names, and shot at by other US soldiers. David Oshiro was a Japanese American soldier in Vietnam. He was wounded, but other American soldiers were hesitant to put him in the medical helicopter. "I had to whip out my dog tag and say, 'I'm an American.' They will get all the Black and white guys before they get the Asians out."

Making Strides in Politics

Although Asians faced a lot of discrimination during the Vietnam War, they also worked toward more political representation. In 1957 Dalip Singh Saund became the first Asian American to be elected to the US House of Representatives. Two years later, Hiram Fong of Hawaii became the first Asian American elected to the US Senate. In 1965 Hawaii elected Patsy Mink to the House of Representatives, making her the first Asian American woman and the first woman of color to serve in Congress.

Mink is also famous for being the primary author of Title IX. Title IX is a law that prohibits gender discrimination in any educational institution that receives funding from the federal government. After Mink died in 2002, Congress renamed Title IX the Patsy T. Mink Equal Opportunity in Education Act.

Current Issues

Asians have made great social strides since the end of the Vietnam War. For example, while only 42 percent of white Americans have college degrees, 60 percent of Asian Americans do. Many Asian American women earn wages almost as high as white men, who on average make the most of anyone in the US. And there are more Asian Americans in Congress than ever before.

But Asians still face many challenges. Asians are often treated as model minorities. The model minority myth is the stereotype that certain marginalized populations, such as Asian Americans, are smarter, more hard-working, and more successful than others. Not only does this myth unnecessarily pit people of color against one another, but it also ignores the differences between different Asian cultures. For example, in 2021 the median income for an Indian American family was $119,000, but the median for a Burmese American family was just $44,000. In fact, Asians have the widest income differences among all US racial groups. These large gaps show the inaccuracy of assuming that all Asians share the exact same experiences.

Several organizations are actively working to challenge and take apart the model minority myth and instead celebrate their individual histories, cultures, and stories. Advocacy groups such as the Asian Americans Advancing Justice, Asian American Legal Defense and Education Fund, and National Asian Pacific Women's Forum all work to challenge stereotypes and promote the recognition of diverse Asian American experiences. Gold House is a group of Asian cultural leaders amplifying voices in mainstream media. They advocate for greater representation and accurate portrayals of Asian cultures and stories in the media.

On April 4, 2021, hundreds of people marched through New York City's Times Square to protest racism and hate crimes against Asians.

Throughout North America, Asian people also still face anti-Asian hate and discrimination. In the US and Canada, this hatred became especially clear when the COVID-19 pandemic began in 2020. Because the disease was first detected in China, many people blamed Asians for the pandemic. Hate crimes against Asians rose sharply. In response to these hate crimes, Asian American activists banded together to protest the treatment. The organization Stop AAPI (Asian American and Pacific Islander) Hate was formed to work toward racial equity and justice. People also posted on social media using the hashtag #StopAsianHate in support of Asian Americans.

Movements such as #StopAsianHate show how Asians can work together—and with other groups—to work for justice. Since they arrived in North America, Asians have faced a variety of obstacles. But they have found their way and continue to fight for justice.

People attend a Stop Asian Hate candlelight vigil in Alhambra, California, in 2021. The vigil was to show solidarity with Asian American communities in Los Angeles and throughout the US.

REFLECT

How can social media play a role in fighting for racial justice?

CONCLUSION
Creating the Future

When thinking about the future of racial justice, there is much to consider and much work that needs to be done. Each North American country has individuals and groups that promote racist agendas that may undo the social and legislative progress that people of color have made. People of color also continue to face discrimination such as hate crimes and police violence.

REFLECT
Have you seen any examples of racial injustice near you? What did you do? What will you do next time?

But North America is more multicultural than ever before. Being exposed to diverse people of different races and ethnicities may make people more understanding of one another. Perhaps interacting with people from different groups will promote unity and decrease discrimination.

Technology can play a role in the fight for racial justice too. Cell phones and social media have made it much easier for people to record and display hate crimes, hate speech, and police violence. Technology can also facilitate community collaboration, allowing people to share experiences, discuss issues, and organize events for racial justice.

History teaches us patterns. We can see how people of color have been treated over several decades or centuries. While it's unlikely that the same thing will happen more than once, people will likely try to harm the same groups in a continued effort to make people of color feel powerless or afraid. Whenever you see the patterns of history repeating, pay attention. Like any kind of justice, racial justice doesn't happen overnight. But anyone can work to create the future they want to see.

What You Can Do

Do you want to help create racial justice in your community? Promoting racial justice in your community takes education, activism, and building positive relationships. Some things you can do include:
- Start open and honest conversations about race in your community or school. Create safe places for people to share their experiences. Listen respectfully to different voices in your community.
- Help people feel welcomed and valued at any gathering or event at your school or in your community.
- Think about your own beliefs. Our beliefs about racial justice that we learned when we were younger can influence how we work for racial justice today.
- Support local businesses owned by people of color.
- Share your knowledge about racial justice with your friends and family.

GLOSSARY

accountability: a willingness of individuals, organizations, or institutions to accept responsibility for their actions, decisions, and their consequences

activist: someone who actively campaigns for social or political change, often by participating in protests, demonstrations, or other forms of direct action

advocate: to support or argue for a cause or policy. An advocate is one who supports or promotes the interests of a cause or group.

assimilate: to become part of a new culture or society, adopting its customs, traditions, or ways of life

bias: when someone has a preference or prejudice that affects how they think or act, sometimes without even realizing it

colonization: when a country establishes control over a group of people or an area outside its borders

colony: a settlement that a country establishes outside of its territory

deport: to expel a person from a country

diaspora: the scattering of a group of people who share a common origin, identity, or cultural heritage

discrimination: a prejudiced or biased outlook, action, or treatment

ethnicity: describes a group that shares a similar language, history, and culture but not necessarily a race

expedition: a journey for a specific purpose such as for exploration, scientific research, or adventure

incarceration camp: a facility where people, often in large groups, are detained and held against their will, typically during times of war, conflict, or political unrest

Indigenous: related to the first people to live in a particular place

Inuit: Indigenous peoples living in the Arctic regions of Canada, Greenland, Alaska, and Siberia

land acknowledgment: a formal statement recognizing and honoring Indigenous peoples who inhabited and cared for the land upon which an event or activity takes place

literacy: the ability to read, write, and comprehend information

lobby: to influence lawmakers to create certain laws or policies that benefit an individual's or group's interests

lynching: an act of putting someone to death, usually by hanging, without a legal trial

marginalized: a social or economic process where individuals or groups are pushed to the edges or margins of society and excluded from the mainstream

Métis: an Indigenous group in Canada with mixed Indigenous and European ancestry, often tracing their roots to First Nations and French Canadian heritage

monarch: a king or queen who holds supreme authority over a nation or territory

nationality: refers to the country where a person lives or was born

reparations: compensation made to individuals, groups, or countries that have suffered from historical injustices, often in the form of financial payments

segregation: the enforced separation of individuals or groups based on certain characteristics such as race, ethnicity, religion, or gender

social worker: a person who is trained to help individuals, families, and communities cope with various challenges

stewardship: traditional and contemporary practices of caring for and managing the natural environment that ensures its sustainability for future generations

trauma: a term used to describe deeply distressing or harmful experiences that can have lasting effects on a person's mental or emotional well-being

xenophobia: a fear or hatred of people from a different country or culture, often leading to discrimination or hostility toward them

SOURCE NOTES

13 "The President . . . into their country.": Jeffrey Ostler, "Was Indian Removal Genocidal?" *Panorama: Expansive Views from the Journal of the Early Republic*, August 4, 2020, http://thepanorama.shear.org/2020/08/04/was-indian-removal-genocidal/.

14 "Kill the Indian . . . save the man.": "Captain Richard H. Pratt on the Education of Native Americans," Carlisle Indian School Digital Resource Center, CIS Resources, accessed January 20, 2024, https://carlisleindian.dickinson.edu/sites/default/files/docs-resources/CIS-Resources_PrattSpeechExcerptShort_0.pdf.

22 "[T]he whole ship's . . . which many died.": Olaudah Equiano, "Is It Not Enough that We Are Torn From Our Country and Friends? Olaudah Equiano Describes the Horrors of the Middle Passage, 1780s," American Social History Project / Center for Media and Learning (Graduate Center, CUNY) and the Roy Rosenzweig Center for History and New Media (George Mason University), accessed January 16, 2024, https://historymatters.gmu.edu/d/6372/.

23 "Can't see in . . . see at night.": "By the Sweat of Our Brows: Slave Tasks," Cultural Landscape of the Plantation, accessed February 21, 2024, https://www2.gwu.edu/~folklife/bighouse/panel9.html.

50 "I had to . . . the Asians out.": Julie Chao, "Asian American Vets Can't Forget Vietnam War Racism," SFGate, April 2, 1999, https://www.sfgate.com/news/article/asian-american-vets-can-t-forget-vietnam-war-3090545.php.

SELECTED BIBLIOGRAPHY

Banks, Sandy. "The Birth of Chicano Studies." *California State University Los Angeles Magazine*. Accessed April 9, 2024. https://www.calstatelamagazine.com/features/the-birth-of-chicano-studies.

Jones, Janelle, John Schmitt, and Valerie Wilson. "50 Years After the Kerner Commission." Economic Policy Institute, February 26, 2018. https://www.epi.org/publication/50-years-after-the-kerner-commission/.

Jones, Seth G. "The Rise of Far-Right Extremism in the United States." Center for Strategic and International Studies, November 7, 2018. https://www.csis.org/analysis/rise-far-right-extremism-united-states.

Joseph, Bob. "Indigenous or Aboriginal: Which Is Correct?" Canadian Broadcasting Corporation News, September 21, 2016. https://www.cbc.ca/news/indigenous/indigenous-aboriginal-which-is-correct-1.3771433.

Kennedy, Lesley. "Building the Transcontinental Railroad: How 20,000 Chinese Immigrants Made It Happen." History, April 23, 2024. https://www.history.com/news/transcontinental-railroad-chinese-immigrants.

Mintz, Steven. "Historical Context: Facts about the Slave Trade and Slavery." Gilder Lehrman Institute of American History. Accessed January 2, 2024. https://www.gilderlehrman.org/history-resources/teacher-resources/historical-context-facts-about-slave-trade-and-slavery.

Ortegon, Mira. "Latino Communities on the Front Lines of Voter Suppression." Brennan Center for Justice, January 14, 2022. https://www.brennancenter.org/our-work/analysis-opinion/latino-communities-front-lines-voter-suppression.

Pruitt, Sarah. "How the Black Power Movement Influenced the Civil Rights Movement." History, July 27, 2023. https://www.history.com/news/black-power-movement-civil-rights.

Ruiz, Neil G., Luis Noe-Bustamante, and Sono Shah. "Diverse Cultures and Shared Experiences Shape Asian American Identities." Pew Research Center, May 8, 2023. https://www.pewresearch.org/race-ethnicity/2023/05/08/diverse-cultures-and-shared-experiences-shape-asian-american-identities/.

Schimmer, Russell. "Hispaniola." Yale University Genocide Studies Program. Accessed January 12, 2024. https://gsp.yale.edu/case-studies/colonial-genocides-project/hispaniola.

Wu, Katherine J. "First Americans Arrived At Least 16,000 Years Ago, and Probably By Boat." *NOVA*, Public Broadcasting Service, August 29, 2019. https://www.pbs.org/wgbh/nova/article/coopers-ferry-first-americans/.

FURTHER INFORMATION

Books

Goldsmith, Connie, and Kiyo Sato. *Kiyo Sato: From a WWII Japanese Internment Camp to a Life of Service*. Minneapolis: Twenty-First Century Books, 2021.
This book tells the story of living in a Japanese incarceration camp, describing why the incarceration happened and how it impacted Kiyo Sato and her family.

Jewell, Tiffany, and Aurélia Durand. *This Book Is Anti-Racist: 20 Lessons on How to Wake Up, Take Action, and Do the Work*. London: Frances Lincoln Children's Books, 2020.
This interactive workbook invites teens to explore and understand racism. It includes activities, reflections, and lessons to inspire young readers to become actively anti-racist.

Nichols, Hedreich, Leigh Ann Erickson, and Kelisa Wing. *Racial Justice in America: Topics for Change*. Ann Arbor: Sleeping Bear Press, 2021.
This book explores current questions around race and how to approach racial issues with open eyes and minds.

Olson, Elsie. *Crossing Borders: Navigating Immigration in North America*. Minneapolis: Twenty-First Century Books, 2025.
This book explores the multifaceted landscape of immigration in North America. It invites readers to reflect on the historical context, sociopolitical dynamics, and contemporary challenges of human migration, ensuring a deeper understanding of this complex topic.

Reynolds, Jason, and Ibram X. Kendi. *Stamped: Racism, Antiracism, and You: A Remix of the National Book Award-winning Stamped from the Beginning*. New York: Little, Brown Books for Young Readers, 2020.
This adaptation of Ibram X. Kendi's *Stamped from the Beginning* provides an accessible and engaging history of racism in America. Jason Reynolds delivers a compelling narrative that encourages critical thinking about the impact of racism on society.

Wray-Lake, Laura, Elan C. Hope, and Laura S. Abrams. *Young Black Changemakers and the Road to Racial Justice*. Cambridge: Cambridge University Press, 2024.
This book tells the stories of how Black youth become changemakers and how a larger purpose drives them to improve the world for Black people.

Websites

Chinese Railroad Workers in North America Project
https://web.stanford.edu/group/chineserailroad/cgi-bin/website/
This website, hosted by Stanford University, explores the stories and experiences of the Chinese immigrant workers who built the US Transcontinental Railroad.

Learning for Justice
https://www.learningforjustice.org/topics/race-ethnicity
This website works with students, teachers, and communities to advance the human rights of all people. They focus on culture and climate, leadership, and community engagement.

National Association for the Advancement of Colored People (NAACP)
https://naacp.org/
With its mission of advancing civil rights and advocating for the rights of African Americans, this organization provides resources and educational materials related to civil rights issues.

National Museum of African American History and Culture, Talking About Race
https://nmaahc.si.edu/learn/talking-about-race
The website has an online portal designed to help individuals, families, and communities discuss racism, racial identity, and the way these two forces shape society.

Racial Equity Tools
https://www.racialequitytools.org/
A place where individuals and groups can find support in working to achieve racial equality. It offers tools, research, tips, and ideas for people who want to work toward racial justice.

The 1619 Project
https://www.nytimes.com/interactive/2019/08/14/magazine/1619-america-slavery.html
This ambitious project aims to reframe US history through the lens of slavery by telling the stories of enslaved Black Americans and exploring how their arrival in colonial America impacted and shaped the United States.

INDEX

activists, 16–17, 30–31, 40–43, 53
    African Americans, 30–31
    Asian American, 53
    Indigenous, 16–17
    Latine, 40–43
African, 5, 18–31, 37, 49
    Americans, 18–31, 37, 49
    culture, 19
    descendants, 5, 18–20, 30–31
    diaspora, 18–31
    enslavement, 18–19, 21–24, 28, 31
        See also under enslavement: African
Afro-Canadians, 19–20, 24, 26
Afro-Latines, 39
Afro-Mexicans, 19–20
American Indian Movement, 16
Asian, 5, 44–53
    advocacy groups, 51, 53
    Americans, 44–51, 53
    culture, 47, 51
    immigrants, 44–47
    North Americans, 44–53
    peoples, 5, 44–53
    rights of, 45–47
    terms of, 47
Assembly of First Nations, 16

Black Panthers, 28, 40
Black Power movement, 20, 28
boarding schools. *See* Indigenous boarding schools
Brown v. Board of Education, 26

Canada, 8, 12, 14–15, 18, 20, 23–24, 26–27, 35, 41–46, 49, 53
    Asians living in, 44–47, 49, 53
    child removal policies in, 14–15
    government of, 15, 26, 45–46
    immigration to, 35, 42–46
    Latines living in, 35, 41–43
    slavery in, 23–24
    voting restrictions in, 24, 45
        See also voting: restrictions in Canada
Chavez, Cesar, 41
Chinese, 44–47
    Americans, 46–47
    Canadians, 45–46
    community, 44, 46
    immigrants, 44–47
    workers, 45
Chinese Exclusion Act, 46–47
    of Canada, 46
    of US, 46–47
civil rights, 25–28, 31, 49
    Civil Rights Act of 1964, 25, 27
    Civil Rights Movement in US, 26–28
    laws, 25–27
    movement in Canada. *See* Rights Revolution
Civil War, 20, 24
Columbus, Christopher, 8, 10, 19, 32

discrimination, 5, 26–28, 31–32, 36–37, 42–43, 45–47, 50, 53–54
    African American, 26–28, 31, 37
    Asian, 45–47, 50, 53
    gender, 50
    Latine, 32, 36–37, 42–43

enslavement, 8, 10, 15, 18–19, 21–24, 28, 31
    African, 18–19, 21–24, 28, 31
    Indigenous, 8, 10, 15, 19

First Nations. *See under* Indigenous peoples: First Nations
Flanagan, Peggy, 17
Fong, Hiram, 50

Haaland, Deb, 17
Huerta, Dolores, 41

Immigration Act of 1917, 47
Immigration Act of 1924, 47
Indigenous boarding schools, 14–15
Indigenous peoples, 5–17, 19
   contributions to world food supply, 9
   culture, 6–7, 13–15
   First Nations, 8, 15–16
   land loss, 10–16
   rights, 17

Japanese, 38–39, 48–50
   Americans, 38–39, 48–50
   incarceration camps, 48–49
   Japanese-Mexican Labor Association, 38–39
Jim Crow laws. *See under* segregation: laws

King, Martin Luther, Jr., 27–29

Land Back Movement, 16–17
Latine, 32, 34–42
   Americans, 32, 35–43
   Canadians, 35, 41–43
   dropout rate, 42
   immigration, 35–38, 42–43
   segregation, 37
   terms for, 34
   workers' rights, 38–39, 41
   youth activism, 40

Malcolm X, 27–28
Mexican-American War, 33
Mexican Revolution, 36
Middle Passage, 21–22
Mink, Patsy, 50

National Association for the Advancement of Colored People (NAACP), 20, 26, 31
   Legal Defense Fund, 31
National Indian Brotherhood. *See* Assembly of First Nations

Obama, Barack, 28, 42

Parks, Rosa, 27
Parsons, Lucy Gonzales, 39
Porvenir, Texas, 36–37

reparations, 31, 48–49
Rights Revolution, 26–27

segregation, 24–28, 37–38, 45
   laws, 24, 27
   of African Americans, 24–28
   of Asians, 45
   of Latines, 37–38
Shelby County v. Holder, 28
slavery. *See* enslavement
Sotomayor, Sonia, 41–42
Spanish-American War, 35
Stop Asian Hate Movement, 53

Till, Emmet, 26
Trail of Tears, 12–13
Transcontinental Railroad, 44–45
Treaty of Guadalupe Hildago, 33, 36
Treaty of Paris, 35
Triangular Trade, 21

US Indian Removal Act, 12–13

Vargas, Jose Antonio, 42–43
Vietnam War, 49–51
voting, 17, 24, 27–28, 31, 37, 45
   laws, 17, 27–28, 37, 45
   restrictions in Canada, 24, 45
      See also Canada: voting restrictions in
   rights of African Americans, 24, 27–28, 31
   rights of Afro-Canadians, 24
   rights of Asians, 45
   rights of Indigenous peoples, 17
   rights of Latines, 37
   suppression, 5, 17, 24, 28, 37, 45
Voting Rights Act of 1965, 27–28

World War I, 47
World War II, 48–49

ABOUT THE AUTHOR

Nareissa Smith is a lawyer, former law professor, journalist, writer, and history educator. She attended Spelman College and Howard University School of Law. Originally from Michigan, Smith has lived in many places across the US. In her rare downtime, she enjoys spending time with her family.

PHOTO ACKNOWLEDGMENTS

The images in this book are used with the permission of:
© master1305/Adobe Stock, p. 5; © Library of Congress, pp. 7, 9, 11, 20, 29, 39, 41, 50; © Wikimedia Commons, pp. 12 (Trail of Tears routes), 14, 25, 27, 34, 40; © Imago/Alamy Photo, p. 16; © rtguest/iStockphoto, p. 21 (base map); © British Library/Wikimedia Commons, p. 22; © Scott Muthersbaugh/AP Images, p. 30; © Everett Collection/Shutterstock Images, p. 33; © Xinhua/Alamy Photo, p. 35; © Cedar Attanasio/AP Images, p. 37; © Chuck Kennedy/National Archives and Records Administration, p. 42; © Allison Bailey/Alamy Photo, p. 43; © Golden Spike National Historic Park, p. 45; © Design Pics Inc/Alamy Photo, p. 46; © Everett Collection Historical/Alamy Photo, p. 48; © Sang Cheng/Shutterstock Images, p. 52; © ZUMA Press, Inc./Alamy Photo, p. 53.

Cover Photo: © Xavier Lorenzo/Adobe Stock

Design Elements: © Ezhevika/Shutterstock Images